The Truck Parade

Story by Jenny Giles

Illustrations by Rachel Tonkin

"Our truck will be the best one
in the parade," said Luke to his dad,
as he cleaned one of the huge wheels.

Luke was at the truck yard,
helping his father
wash their new truck.

"It's looking good!" said Dad.
"Those wheels are really shining."

"I can even see my face
in this one!" grinned Luke.

The truck parade was going to start
from the fair grounds,
and Luke wanted his dad's truck
to be the brightest
and shiniest of all.

As Luke finished cleaning
the last wheel,
Bill came out of the office.
He called to Luke's dad,
"Can you take a load
to the new supermarket?
Your truck is the only one here
at the moment."

Luke's dad looked at his watch.
"Yes," he said.
"That won't take too long.
If I leave now,
there will still be enough time
for us to get to the fair grounds."

"Thanks," said Bill.
"Luke can stay in the office
until you get back."

Luke watched his dad
climb into the cab.
"Don't get our truck dirty!"
he shouted.

"I won't," Dad called back.
"It's a nice sunny day."

But when Dad arrived back
at the truck yard,
the wheels were all wet and muddy.
Luke stared at them in surprise.
"What happened?" he cried.

"I had to go through some road work,"
said Dad.
"The wheels got covered in mud,
and the truck got splashed.
We'll have to wash it again."

"But we'll be too late for the parade!"
cried Luke.

"There will be just enough time
to get there if we start now,"
said Dad. "Come on!"

Bill got the hose out
and helped them wash the truck.

As they finished, Luke groaned,
"I'm tired of cleaning wheels!
I've had to do them all **twice**."

"You've done a great job!" said Dad.
"The truck is all bright
and shiny again. Now, let's go!"

Luke climbed up into the cab
and looked out the window.
In the distance,
he could see the fair grounds.

Then he saw a long line of trucks,
moving slowly along the road.

"Oh no!" cried Luke.
"We are too late.
The parade has started already."
He was very disappointed.

Dad and Bill ran to the fence.
They stared at the line of trucks.

TRUCK PARADE

13

Suddenly, Luke shouted, "Dad!
The parade is going to come
right past us.
We could join on to the end!"

"I think we could!" said Dad.
"Let's give it a try."
He climbed up into the cab
and drove to the gate.

Luke watched all the huge trucks
driving past.

Then a police officer saw them waiting,
and waved them on
to the end of the line.

Luke grinned at Dad.
"I've seen all the trucks in the parade," he said, "and ours looks the best."

"So it should," laughed Dad.
"It must be **twice** as bright and shiny as any of the others!"